SLAB *Pies*

AND OTHER BIG PAN DESSERTS

ONE RECIPE. ONE BIG PAN. PLENTY OF DESSERT.

This is it – the easy way to make dessert for parties, potlucks, and other get-togethers. Each slab of pie, cake, or bars will serve 15 to 36. That's a whole lot of goodness in a single pan, and you only have to bake once!

Use the helpful **Quick Tips** *throughout this book to make your crowd-pleasing desserts even more incredible!.*

ISBN-13: 978-1-56383-566-7
Item #7143

**Printed in the USA
by G&R Publishing Co.**

Distributed By:

507 Industrial Street
Waverly, IA 50677

www.cqbookstore.com

gifts@cqbookstore.com

 CQ Products

 CQ Products

 @cqproducts

 @cqproducts

Use a standard 10 x 15 x 1" jelly roll pan *(sheet pan)* for all these desserts. *(Give or take an inch on any side, but be sure the pan is 1" deep.)* Prepare cakes and bars as you would for smaller pans, using cooking spray to grease the pans, if directed. For pies, follow these tips.

1. Make homemade pastry with one of our recipes, or use packaged mixes or two refrigerated crusts. Swap out the crusts and fillings based on your time and tastes.

2. Cut in sliced butter, shortening, or lard with a pastry blender or food processor. For the flakiest crusts, you want to break up the fat into small pieces and coat them in the flour mixture.

3. Use just enough cold liquid to hold pastry dough together and don't over-work it.

4. Generously flour a work surface and rolling pin *(a pastry cloth works especially well)*, and roll dough from the center out in all directions until thin and even.

5. To move pastry to the pan, gently fold it in half or roll it around the rolling pin; center pastry over the pan, then unfold or unroll it. Ease it into the pan without stretching and press it up the sides, leaving a 1" overhang that can be folded and crimped.

6. For a double-crust pie, fold the bottom and top edges together; crimp the crust in a decorative pattern or press together with a fork.

7. Use a dab of water to patch dough or fasten layers together.

8. If a crust must be prebaked before adding a filling *("blind baking")*, either poke fork holes in the bottom and sides to prevent bubbling or use pie weights *(see Quick Tip on page 9)*. Then fill and chill the pie, or fill and return to the oven to finish baking *(as for meringue)*.

Glazed Apple Pie Squares

Crust

2¾ C. flour
1 tsp. salt
1 C. butter, sliced
1 egg yolk
⅓ C. milk or half & half
1 C. crushed cornflakes

Filling

9 C. thinly sliced, peeled
   apples (we used 10
   medium Jonathans)

1 C. sugar
1½ tsp. cinnamon
½ tsp. ground nutmeg

Toppings & Glaze

1 egg white, lightly beaten
2 T. cinnamon-sugar
1 C. powdered sugar
½ tsp. vanilla
1 to 2 T. milk

For the crust, combine flour and salt in a large bowl. Cut in butter until coarse crumbs form. Combine egg yolk and milk, then gradually add to flour mixture and work with hands until dough forms. Divide dough in half.

Preheat the oven. Roll one piece of dough into a thin 14 x 19" rectangle. Transfer to a 10 x 15 x 1" pan and press into corners and up the sides, leaving a 1" overhang. Sprinkle cornflakes over the bottom and set aside.

Put all filling ingredients into a bowl and toss to mix; spoon mixture into the crust. Roll the remaining dough into another large rectangle and place over apple filling. Moisten the edges, pinch crusts together, and crimp as desired around rim of pan.

Brush egg white over the top crust and sprinkle with cinnamon-sugar. Bake as indicated, until golden brown.

For the glaze, whisk together powdered sugar, vanilla, and enough milk to make a drizzling consistency. Drizzle over warm pastry and cool completely. *Serves 20-24*

350°   45-55 min.

Strawberry-Lemonade Fingers

Preheat the oven and line a 10 x 15 x 1" pan with greased foil. Whisk together 1¼ C. melted butter, 1¼ C. sugar, and ⅔ C. brown sugar. Stir in 3¾ C. flour and ½ tsp. salt until crumbly. Set aside 1 C. of the mixture for the topping; press the remainder into the prepped pan for the crust.

Whisk together 2 eggs, 1¼ C. vanilla Greek yogurt *(or sour cream)*, ¾ C. sugar, 5 T. lemon juice, and 1 T. vanilla until smooth. Whisk in ½ C. plus 2 T. flour and a pinch of salt until well blended. Spread filling over crust.

In a big bowl, combine 5 C. diced fresh strawberries, ¾ C. sugar, 5 T. lemon juice, 1½ T. lemon zest, and 2 T. cornstarch *(add more cornstarch if berries are extra juicy)*. Spoon berry mixture over the filling and sprinkle with the set-aside topping. Bake as indicated, until filling is bubbly. Let cool at least 2 hours or overnight, or chill before serving. *Serves 35*

 350°  60-70 min.

Favorite Pumpkin Bars

Preheat the oven and grease a 10 x 15 x 1" pan. Whisk together 1 C. vegetable oil, 4 eggs, and 1¾ C. sugar until blended. Stir in 2 C. flour, 1 tsp. baking soda, 2 tsp. baking powder, 2 tsp. cinnamon, ½ tsp. ground cloves, and ½ tsp. salt until smooth and well mixed. Mix in 1 (15 oz.) can pumpkin puree. Spread batter in the prepped pan and bake as indicated or until cake tests done with a toothpick. Let cool completely.

For the frosting, beat together ½ (8 oz.) pkg. softened cream cheese and ½ C. softened butter on medium speed until smooth. Beat in 2 tsp. vanilla. Gradually beat in 2¼ C. powdered sugar until smooth. Spread or pipe frosting over the cooled bars; if you'd like, sprinkle with cinnamon. Store in the refrigerator. *Serves 25-30*

Chocolate Cream Slab Pie

Crust

1 (9 to 11 oz.) pkg. pie crust
  mix *(for 2 crusts)*
Water as directed on package

Filling

2 C. sugar
⅓ C. cornstarch
Pinch of salt
1½ C. heavy cream
1½ C. buttermilk

8 egg yolks
8 oz. bittersweet or
  unsweetened baking
  chocolate, chopped
2 T. butter, sliced
2 tsp. vanilla

Toppings

2 C. heavy cream
⅓ C. powdered sugar
Chocolate candy, shavings,
  or sprinkles, optional

 350° 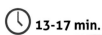 13-17 min.

Preheat the oven as directed for pie crust mix and follow package directions to prepare pastry dough for two crusts with the mix and water.

On a floured surface, roll out the dough to make a 14 x 19" rectangle. Transfer to a 10 x 15 x 1" pan, pressing dough into the corners and up the sides and leaving a 1" overhang. Fold under and crimp dough around the rim as desired. Poke fork holes all over the bottom and sides of crust *(or use pie weights following instructions below)*. Bake as indicated, until lightly browned. Cool completely.

For the filling, combine sugar, cornstarch, and salt in a large saucepan. Whisk in the cream, buttermilk, and egg yolks. Place over medium heat, stirring constantly until mixture thickens and just comes to a boil, 6 to 8 minutes. Remove from heat and stir in the chocolate, butter, and vanilla until melted and smooth. Let cool 10 to 15 minutes, then place plastic wrap on the surface of filling and chill for 30 minutes. Pour filling into crust and refrigerate about 4 hours.

Before serving, prepare the topping. Beat the cream in a chilled bowl with chilled beaters on medium speed until soft peaks form; beat in powdered sugar. Spread over filling and garnish with chocolate as desired. Store leftovers in the fridge. *Serves 20*

Quick Tip

*To use **PIE WEIGHTS** when prebaking an empty pie shell, fit the bottom crust into the pan and line with foil or parchment paper. Fill with dried beans or purchased pie weights and then bake as directed. Remove the liner and beans and finish assembling the pie.*

Peach Crumb Slab Pie

Crust & Toppings

1½ C. quick oats
3 C. flour
¾ C. sugar
1½ C. cold butter
5 to 8 T. ice water
2 T. cinnamon-sugar

Filling

3 (29 oz.) cans plus
   1 (15 oz.) can sliced
   peaches, drained
¼ C. plus 2 T. sugar
½ C. flour
1 to 2 tsp. cinnamon
½ tsp. ground nutmeg
¼ tsp. salt

To make the crust and topping mixture, whisk together the oats, flour, and sugar. Grate the butter into the dry ingredients and mix it in with a pastry blender or your fingertips until crumbly. Work in 1 tablespoon water at a time until dough can be pressed into a ball. Wrap in plastic wrap and chill 30 to 60 minutes.

In a big bowl, stir together all filling ingredients; set aside.

Preheat the oven. On a floured surface, roll out ⅔ of the chilled dough into a 13 x 18" rectangle. Carefully transfer dough to a 10 x 15 x 1" pan, pressing it into the corners and up the sides, and crimping around rim as desired. Spoon the set-aside filling into the crust. Crumble the remaining dough evenly over filling and sprinkle with cinnamon-sugar. Bake as indicated, until topping and crust are golden brown and filling is bubbly. Garnish pieces as you like. *Serves 15-20*

350°   45-55 min.

Scotchie Crunch Cake

Preheat the oven and lightly grease a 10 x 15 x 1" pan; line bottom with parchment paper. In a saucepan, heat 1 C. milk and 2 T. butter until steaming; let cool. In a mixing bowl, beat 4 eggs, 1 C. sugar, and 1 C. brown sugar on medium speed until thick and pale, 3 to 5 minutes; beat in 1½ tsp. vanilla. Gradually beat in 2 C. flour, 1 tsp. baking powder, and ¼ tsp. salt, then slowly beat in cooled milk mixture. Pour batter into the prepped pan and bake as indicated, until cake tests done. Cool completely.

For the frosting, melt ½ C. unsalted butter in a saucepan over medium-low heat. Add ⅔ C. brown sugar; bring to a boil, then cook and stir 2 more minutes. Whisk in ½ C. heavy cream and ½ tsp. salt; stir and boil 1 minute longer. Remove from heat and cool 5 minutes, stirring often. Beat in 2 tsp. vanilla and 2 C. powdered sugar. Spread over cake and sprinkle with toffee pieces. *Serves 24*

 350°  20-25 min.

Chocolate-Cherry Bars

Preheat the oven and line a 10 x 15 x 1" pan with greased foil. In the microwave, melt 2 oz. unsweetened baking chocolate, stirring until smooth; set aside to cool.

In a big mixing bowl, combine 1 (8 oz.) pkg. softened cream cheese, ¾ C. softened butter, and 1 C. sugar; beat until creamy. Beat in 2 eggs and 1 tsp. vanilla. Add 1¼ C. flour, ½ tsp. baking soda, and ½ tsp. salt and mix well. Beat in the set-aside chocolate, then fold in 1 C. drained and chopped maraschino cherries *(reserve juice)* and ½ C. chopped sliced almonds. Spread batter in the prepped pan and bake as indicated, until bars test done.

In a medium bowl, microwave 2 oz. unsweetened baking chocolate until melted. Stir in 1 C. sifted powdered sugar, 2 T. half & half, 2 T. cherry juice, and ½ tsp. vanilla until smooth. Drizzle over dessert and sprinkle with more almonds. Cool completely. *Serves 36*

 350°  22-25 min.

Coconut Cream Slab Pie

Crust

1 (9 to 11 oz.) pkg. pie crust
   mix *(for 2 crusts)*
Water as directed on package

Filling

1½ C. sugar
½ C. cornstarch
5 C. half & half
8 egg yolks
1½ to 2 C. sweetened
   flaked coconut

¼ C. plus 2 T. cream
   of coconut
2 T. butter, sliced
1 T. clear vanilla

Meringue

8 egg whites *(at room
   temperature)*
1 tsp. cream of tartar
1½ tsp. vanilla
½ C. plus 2 T. sugar
½ C. toasted coconut

 425° 24-27 min.

Preheat the oven as directed for pie crust mix and follow package directions to prepare pastry dough for two crusts with the mix and water.

On a floured surface, roll out the dough to make a 14 x 19" rectangle. Transfer to a 10 x 15 x 1" pan, pressing dough into the corners and up the sides and leaving a 1" overhang. Crimp dough around rim as desired. Poke fork holes all over the bottom and sides of crust. Bake 9 to 12 minutes, until lightly browned. Let cool.

Reduce oven temperature to 325°. For the filling, combine sugar and cornstarch in a large saucepan. Slowly whisk in the half & half and egg yolks. Cook over medium heat until mixture almost comes to a boil, stirring constantly. Reduce heat; cook and stir 2 more minutes. Remove from heat and stir in the coconut, cream of coconut, butter, and vanilla until well mixed; set aside and keep warm.

For the meringue, combine egg whites, cream of tartar, and vanilla in large mixing bowl and beat on medium speed about 1 minute, until foamy. Gradually beat in the sugar on high speed until sugar dissolves and stiff glossy peaks form, 3 to 5 minutes.

To assemble, pour warm filling into crust and spread meringue on top, sealing to the crust edges and swirling the top. Sprinkle with toasted coconut *(see Quick Tip below)*. Bake about 15 minutes, until meringue has golden brown peaks. Cool 1 hour and refrigerate at least 3 hours before serving. Store leftovers in the fridge. *Serves 20*

Quick Tip

To **TOAST COCONUT, PECANS, OR WALNUTS**, *cook in a skillet over medium heat until golden brown and fragrant, stirring often. Let cool before using.*

Grasshopper Dessert

Cake

1 (16.25 oz.) pkg. white cake mix

1¼ C. water

⅓ C. vegetable oil

3 egg whites

¼ C. crème de menthe syrup or liqueur

Toppings

1 or 2 (12.8 oz.) jars hot fudge topping

1 (12 oz.) container whipped topping, thawed

3 T. crème de menthe syrup or liqueur

¼ tsp. peppermint extract

Andes mints, chopped

Preheat the oven and grease the bottom only of a 10 x 15 x 1" pan.

To make the cake, combine cake mix, water, oil, and egg whites in a large mixing bowl and beat on low speed for 30 seconds. Increase speed to medium and beat 2 minutes more. Stir in the crème de menthe until well combined. Spread batter in the prepped pan and bake as indicated or until cake tests done with a toothpick. Cool completely.

To top the cake, spread the fudge topping evenly over the cooled cake. Stir together the whipped topping, crème de menthe, and peppermint extract; dollop or spread the mixture evenly over the fudge layer. Refrigerate and garnish with mints before serving.

Serves 20

 350°   20-22 min.

Easy Monster Cookie Bars

Preheat the oven to 350° and grease a 10 x 15 x 1" pan. In a large mixing bowl, beat together ½ C. softened butter, 1 C. sugar, and 1 C. brown sugar on medium speed until smooth. Beat in 1½ C. creamy peanut butter, 3 eggs, and 1 tsp. vanilla until well blended. Add 4½ C. quick oats and 2 tsp. baking soda and mix well.

With a spoon, stir in ¾ C. peanut butter M&Ms, ½ C. mini M&Ms, and 1 C. semi-sweet chocolate chips until well combined. Press mixture into the prepped pan and bake as indicated, until edges begin to brown. Cool completely before cutting. *Serves 24-36*

350°   15-20 min.

Sour Cream Raisin Bars

Preheat the oven and grease a 10 x 15 x 1" pan. In a saucepan over medium heat, simmer 2 C. raisins in ¾ C. water for 5 minutes to soften. Cool 10 minutes, then drain.

Stir together 1¾ C. quick oats, 1¾ C. flour, 1 tsp. baking soda, and 1 C. brown sugar. Cut in 1 C. sliced butter until mixture is crumbly. Press 4 C. of the mixture into the bottom of the prepped pan and reserve the remaining 2 C. for the topping. Bake crust for 10 minutes.

Meanwhile, in a large microwave-safe bowl, mix 1½ C. sugar, 2 T. cornstarch, ½ tsp. cinnamon, ¼ tsp. ground nutmeg, and ½ tsp. salt. Whisk in 2 C. sour cream, 4 egg yolks, and 1 tsp. vanilla; fold in softened raisins. Microwave mixture on high 5 to 7 minutes to thicken, stirring often; pour over the warm crust. Sprinkle with reserved topping and bake 25 minutes more, until lightly browned. Cool completely and sprinkle with powdered sugar. *Serves 24*

 350°  35 min.

Pumpkin Pie for a Crowd

Crust

3⅓ C. flour
1 T. sugar
1 tsp. salt
1 C. canola oil
6 T. milk or half & half
Egg wash (see p. 29)

Filling

2 (15 oz.) cans pumpkin puree
2 C. brown sugar
4 eggs

2¼ C. half & half
2 tsp. vanilla
2½ T. cornstarch
1 T. pumpkin pie spice
½ tsp. cinnamon
½ tsp. salt
⅛ tsp. black pepper
½ to 1 tsp. grated fresh
    gingerroot, optional

Topping

Whipped topping

 375°   40 min.

To make the no-roll crust, combine flour, sugar, and salt in a 10 x 15 x 1" pan and mix well with a fork. In a measuring cup, whisk the oil and milk together. Pour the liquid over the flour mixture in pan and stir until completely moistened. Pat the dough into the pan with your fingers, working it up the sides of pan first and then across the bottom. Crimp dough around the rim and brush lightly with egg wash. Refrigerate until ready to fill.

Preheat the oven. Combine all the filling ingredients in a very big bowl and whisk together until thick and well blended.

Pour filling into the prepped crust. Bake as indicated or until the filling is only slightly jiggly in the very center. Cool completely before slicing into squares or pie-like wedges. Garnish with dollops of whipped topping or try Spiced Whipped Cream *(see Quick Tip below)*. Store leftovers in the fridge. *Serves 12-24*

Quick Tip

Make this dessert extra-special with homemade **SPICED WHIPPED CREAM**. *Chill a metal bowl and beaters in the freezer for 15 minutes; pour 2 C. cold heavy cream into the bowl and beat until thickened. Gradually beat in ⅓ C. sugar and ¼ tsp. cinnamon extract until soft peaks form. Stir in 1½ tsp. cinnamon and ¼ to ½ tsp. ground nutmeg (or ginger) until blended. Delish!*

Fruit Pizza

Crust

1 (16.5 oz.) tube refrigerated sugar cookie dough

Toppings

2 (8 oz.) pkgs. cream cheese, softened

1 C. powdered sugar

1 tsp. vanilla

1 (8 oz.) container whipped topping, thawed

4 C. fresh fruit *(such as strawberries, kiwifruit, pineapple, blueberries, and raspberries)*

1 (11 oz.) can mandarin oranges, drained

Glaze

1 C. sugar

3 T. cornstarch

1 C. orange juice

¼ C. unsweetened pineapple juice

Preheat the oven. Press the cookie dough into the bottom of a 10 x 15 x 1" pan and bake as indicated, until golden brown. Let cool completely.

In a large mixing bowl, beat together the cream cheese, powdered sugar, and vanilla on medium speed until smooth. Fold in the whipped topping. Spread mixture over the cooled crust and arrange the fresh and canned fruit on top as desired; set aside.

To make the glaze, whisk together the sugar, cornstarch, orange juice, and pineapple juice in a medium saucepan until blended. Bring to a boil over medium heat and cook for 2 minutes or until thickened, stirring constantly. When cool, drizzle over the fruit. Chill or serve at room temperature. Store leftovers in the fridge.

Serves 20-25

350°   10-15 min.

Lime-n-Coconut Bars

Preheat the oven. Combine 2 C. flour, ¼ C. sugar, and ¼ tsp. salt in a medium bowl. Cut in ½ C. plus 2 T. butter *(sliced)* until fine crumbs form. Press the mixture into a 10 x 15 x 1" pan and bake for 15 to 20 minutes, until barely browned.

In another bowl, whisk 4 eggs. Stir in 1 C. finely chopped toasted coconut-flavored almonds *(or lightly salted plain almonds)*, 2 C. brown sugar, and 3 C. sweetened flaked coconut. Spread mixture over the warm crust and bake 25 minutes longer, until set. Set pan on a cooling rack and run a knife around pan edges to loosen.

Meanwhile, to make the glaze, whisk together 2 C. sifted powdered sugar with 3 T. lime juice and 2 tsp. lime zest until smooth. Spread over warm bars and let cool completely before cutting. *Serves 40*

 350° 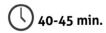 40-45 min.

Boston Cream Freezer Dessert

Line a 10 x 15 x 1" pan with foil and cover the bottom with a layer of graham crackers *(about 14 rectangles)*, breaking some as needed to fit small spaces. In a large bowl, whisk together 3 C. milk, 2 (3.4 oz.) pkgs. vanilla instant pudding mix, and 1 (8 oz.) container whipped topping *(thawed)* until smooth and thickened. Spread the mixture evenly over the crackers. Place another layer of graham crackers over the pudding layer.

For the topping, combine 1 C. sugar, ½ C. butter, ½ C. semi-sweet chocolate chips, ¼ C. milk, and 1 tsp. vanilla in a saucepan over medium heat. Cook and stir until mixture comes to a simmer and everything is melted and smooth. Pour over the top layer of crackers. Freeze at least 4 hours or overnight. Garnish pieces as you like and store any leftovers in the freezer. *Serves 20-24*

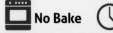 **No Bake**   **Freeze time: 4 hours**

French Silk Slab Pie

Crust

1 (14 to 15 oz.) pkg.
   refrigerated pie crusts
   (2 ct.)

Filling

2 C. unsalted butter, softened

3 C. sugar

4 oz. unsweetened baking
   chocolate, melted & cooled

1 T. vanilla

1 (16 oz.) carton egg
   substitute

Toppings

1 (8 oz.) container whipped
   topping, thawed

1 milk chocolate candy bar

Soften the pie crusts at room temperature as directed on package, then preheat the oven. Unroll both crusts and overlap them in the center of a 10 x 15 x 1" pan. With your hands, press the pastry over the bottom, into the corners, and up the sides of pan, leaving a 1" overhang and patching as needed to make one crust. Crimp dough around the rim as desired and poke fork holes all over the bottom and sides of crust. Bake as indicated or until light brown. Cool completely.

To make the filling, beat the butter and sugar together on medium-high speed in a large mixing bowl until light and fluffy, 6 to 7 minutes. Beat in the chocolate and vanilla until well combined. Add about ½ C. of egg substitute at a time and beat 5 minutes after each addition until all has been added and mixture is smooth *(don't over-beat)*. Cover and chill the filling for 2 to 3 hours. Spread filling evenly over the cooled crust followed by whipped topping. Shave or grate the candy bar over the top before serving. Store any leftovers in the fridge. *Serves 20*

450°   10-12 min.

Blueberry Dazzle Pie

Crust

3⅓ C. flour

1 T. sugar

1½ tsp. salt

1⅓ C. unsalted butter, sliced

1 egg, lightly beaten

1 tsp. white vinegar

7 T. ice water

Filling

4 lbs. frozen blueberries, divided

1½ C. sugar

5 T. water, divided

½ C. cornstarch

Zest of 2 lemons

Scant ½ C. lemon juice

2 tsp. cinnamon

1 tsp. salt

Toppings

Egg wash (see p. 29)

Sugar

375° 45-50 min.

For the crust, combine flour, sugar, and salt in a food processor and pulse until combined. Add the butter and pulse to make coarse crumbs. In a bowl, whisk together the egg, vinegar, and water; sprinkle over flour mixture and pulse until dough comes together. Divide dough in half, flatten, and wrap separately in plastic wrap; refrigerate about 30 minutes.

To make the filling, stir together half the blueberries, sugar, and 2 tablespoons water in a big saucepan over medium heat until sugar dissolves and berries are thawed. In a small bowl, mix cornstarch and remaining 3 tablespoons water; stir into the saucepan and bring mixture to a boil. Cook and stir until sauce is clear, thickened, and reduced; transfer to a large bowl. Stir in the remaining berries, lemon zest and juice, cinnamon, and salt; set aside.

Preheat the oven. On a floured surface, roll out one piece of chilled dough into a 14 x 19" rectangle. Transfer to a 10 x 15 x 1" pan and press dough into the corners and up the sides, leaving a 1" overhang. Pour filling into the crust. Roll remaining dough into another rectangle, big enough to cover pie. Cut designs in the top crust with small cookie cutters. Set crust on pie; fold edges together and crimp around the rim as desired. Brush egg wash over the crust, then arrange cut-outs on top; brush again and sprinkle with sugar. Bake as indicated, until crust is golden brown and filling is bubbly. Let cool before slicing. *Serves 20*

Quick Tip

*To give pie crusts a shiny golden color, brush the top pastry with an **EGG WASH** before baking. To make, simply whisk together 1 egg white (or a whole egg) with 1 tablespoon water or milk; brush on and bake as directed. When brushed over a bottom crust before filling, an egg wash also prevents sogginess.*

Cherry Pie Bars

In a large mixing bowl, beat together 1 C. softened butter and 2 C. sugar on medium speed until creamy. Add 4 eggs, one at a time, beating after each addition. Mix in 1 tsp. vanilla, 1 tsp. almond extract, 3 C. flour and 1 tsp. salt until batter is well combined. Spread 3 C. of the batter in the prepped pan. Spread 2 (21 oz.) cans cherry pie filling over the batter. Drop the remaining batter by spoonful on top of pie filling and bake as indicated, until filling is bubbly and cake tests done and is golden brown around the edges. Let cool.

For the glaze, whisk together 1 C. sifted powdered sugar, ½ tsp. vanilla, ½ tsp. almond extract, and 2 T. milk until smooth. Drizzle over bars before serving. *Serves 20-24*

 350°  40-50 min.

Orange-Sweet Potato Cake

Preheat the oven and grease the bottom only of a 10 x 15 x 1" pan. Zest and juice one medium orange; set the zest aside for the frosting. Add enough water to the juice to equal ½ C. liquid and pour into a large mixing bowl. Add 1 C. cooked mashed sweet potato, 1 (15.25 oz.) pkg. yellow cake mix, 2 tsp. pumpkin pie spice, 1 C. milk, ⅓ C. vegetable oil, and 3 eggs. Beat on low speed for 30 seconds, and then beat on medium speed 2 minutes more. Spread batter in the prepped pan and bake as indicated or until cake tests done. Cool completely.

For the frosting, beat together 1 (8 oz.) pkg. softened cream cheese, ½ C. softened butter, 2½ C. sifted powdered sugar, and 1 tsp. orange extract on medium speed until smooth. Mix in the set-aside orange zest. Spread or pipe frosting on cake. Refrigerate leftovers. *Serves 15-18*

 350°  18-22 min.

Peanut Butter Oat Bars

Crust & Topping

2 C. quick oats
1¾ C. brown sugar
1 C. flour
½ C. whole wheat flour
1 tsp. baking powder
½ tsp. baking soda
1 C. butter, sliced

½ C. chopped peanuts
1 (12 oz.) pkg. milk chocolate chips
1 egg, beaten

Filling

1 (14 oz.) can sweetened condensed milk
⅓ C. creamy peanut butter

Preheat the oven. In a large bowl, stir together the oats, brown sugar, flour, whole wheat flour, baking powder, and baking soda until well combined. Cut in the butter until mixture resembles fine crumbs. Stir in the peanuts. To make the topping, in another bowl, combine 1½ C. of the crumb mixture with the chocolate chips and set aside.

For the crust, stir the egg into the remaining crumb mixture and press into a 10 x 15 x 1" pan. Bake for 15 minutes.

Meanwhile, make the filling. In a medium bowl, mix the sweetened condensed milk and peanut butter until smooth. Pour filling over the hot crust and sprinkle with the set-aside topping. Return to the oven to bake 12 to 15 minutes more or until edges are lightly browned. Cool before cutting. *Serves 24-30*

350° 27-30 min.

Lemon Cheesecake Squares

Preheat the oven. Soften and press 1 (16.5 oz.) roll refrigerated sugar cookie dough into the bottom of a 10 x 15 x 1" pan and set aside. In a large mixing bowl, beat 4 (8 oz.) pkgs. softened cream cheese on medium speed until blended. Beat in ⅔ C. sugar. Add 4 eggs, one at a time, beating on low speed after each addition until filling is smooth and well mixed. Spread filling over the cookie crust in pan.

Spoon 1¼ C. lemon curd into a zippered plastic bag and seal. Cut off ¾" from one corner of bag and squeeze the lemon curd over the filling in five or six thick lines down the length of pan. With the fat end of a wooden skewer, swirl the curd through the filling. Bake as indicated, until filling is almost set in the center. Cool for 30 minutes, then refrigerate at least 1½ hours. If you'd like, sprinkle with powdered sugar before slicing. Store any leftovers in the fridge. *Serves 20-24*

350°   40-45 min.

White Almond Sheet Cake

Preheat the oven and grease and flour a 10 x 15 x 1" pan. In a large mixing bowl, combine 1 (18.25 oz.) pkg. white cake mix, 1 C. flour, 1 C. sugar, and ¾ tsp. salt. Add 1⅓ C. water, 1 C. sour cream, 2 T. vegetable oil, 1 tsp. vanilla, and 1 tsp. almond extract. Beat on low speed about 4 minutes. In another bowl, whisk together 4 egg whites until frothy. Add to cake batter and beat until combined. Pour batter into the prepped pan and bake as indicated, until top is light golden brown and cake tests done with a toothpick. Let cool completely.

For whipped buttercream frosting, beat 1 C. softened butter on medium speed for 3 minutes, until light and fluffy. Beat in 2 tsp. vanilla, 1 tsp. almond extract, 2 T. half & half, and a pinch of salt. Slowly beat in 5 C. powdered sugar. Increase speed slightly and beat 3 more minutes, until fluffy. Spread and/or pipe over cooled cake. *Serves 20-28*

 325°  28-35 min.

Apricot-Cherry Lattice Pie

Crust

3¾ C. flour
2 tsp. sugar
1½ tsp. salt
¾ C. unsalted butter, diced
¾ C. cold lard, diced
7 to 9 T. ice water

Filling

3 (29 oz.) cans apricot halves,
   drained & sliced

2 (16 oz.) cans pitted tart red
   cherries, drained
1 C. sugar
¼ C. plus 2 T. cornstarch

Toppings

Egg wash *(see p. 29)*
Coarse sugar

 375° **40-45 min.**

For the crust, combine the flour, sugar, and salt in a food processor. Add butter and lard, pulsing just until mixture resembles coarse crumbs. Add 7 tablespoons water and pulse until dough clumps together, adding more water by the spoonful as needed *(or transfer dry ingredients to a bowl, stir in the water, and work with hands until dough forms)*. Divide dough in half, wrap in plastic wrap, and refrigerate at least 1 hour *(or up to 3 days)*.

To assemble, roll out one piece of dough on a floured surface to make a 14 x 19" rectangle. Transfer to a 10 x 15 x 1" pan, pressing dough into the corners and up the sides and leaving a 1" overhang. Preheat the oven. Combine all filling ingredients in a big bowl, stirring well; spoon filling into the prepped crust.

Roll remaining dough into another large rectangle. With a pizza cutter, cut dough into long strips, ½" to 1" wide. Weave the strips over the filling as desired to make a lattice top *(see Quick Tip below)*. Trim ends of strips even with the bottom crust, pinch edges together, and crimp as desired. Brush crust and strips with egg wash and sprinkle with sugar. Bake as indicated, until crust is deep golden brown and filling is bubbly. Cool completely. Garnish pieces as you like. *Serves 16-24*

Quick Tip

*To make a **LATTICE CRUST**, lay half the pastry strips diagonally (or vertically) across the entire pie, ¾" apart ("A" strips); fold every other A strip back on itself at the halfway point. Place a long "B" strip in the opposite direction across the first set of strips, then unfold the A strips over this B strip. Fold back the opposite A strips and repeat with a second B strip. Repeat in both directions until lattice is complete.*

Chocolate-Pecan Slab Pie

Crust

2¾ C. flour
2 tsp. salt
2 tsp. sugar
1 C. unsalted butter, sliced
½ C. plus 2 T. buttermilk

Filling

1 (12 oz.) pkg. semi-sweet chocolate chips
3¼ C. pecan halves
6 eggs
1¾ C. brown sugar
1½ C. light corn syrup
¾ C. unsalted butter, melted
1 tsp. salt
2 tsp. vanilla

Preheat the oven to 350°. For the crust, stir together flour, salt, and sugar in a medium bowl. Cut in the butter until mixture resembles coarse crumbs. Add the buttermilk a little at a time, and stir or work with hands until dough forms. Shape into a disk, wrap in plastic wrap, and refrigerate for 30 minutes.

On a floured surface, roll out dough to make a 14 x 19" rectangle. Transfer to a 10 x 15 x 1" pan, pressing dough into the corners and up the sides and leaving a 1" overhang. Fold under and crimp dough as desired around rim. Line crust with foil, fill with pie weights *(see Quick Tip on page 9)*, and prebake for 20 minutes. Carefully remove the foil and weights.

Reduce oven temperature to 325°. For the filling, sprinkle chocolate chips and pecans over the warm crust. Whisk the eggs in a big bowl, then whisk in brown sugar, corn syrup, butter, salt, and vanilla until well blended. Pour filling into the crust. Bake 40 to 50 minutes, until crust is golden brown and filling is set. Shield crust with foil as needed to prevent excess browning. Cool before slicing. Garnish pieces as you like. *Serves 24-28*

350° *(crust)* 325° *(filling)* 60-70 min.

Raspberry Cheesecake Brownies

Preheat the oven and line a 10 x 15 x 1" pan with greased foil. Puree 1½ C. fresh raspberries in a food processor or blender. Strain and discard seeds. Stir ⅓ C. sugar into remaining berry puree and reserve for later use.

In a large bowl, combine 2 (18.3 oz.) pkgs. brownie mix plus the oil, eggs, and water for both boxes as directed; mix well. Spread batter in the prepped pan and set aside.

Melt 6 oz. white baking chocolate in the microwave until smooth; set aside. In a mixing bowl, beat 2 (8 oz.) pkgs. softened cream cheese on medium speed about 1 minute. Beat in 1 C. sugar and 3 eggs; fold in melted white chocolate until combined. Pour cheesecake batter over brownie batter. Spoon the reserved raspberry puree over unbaked cheesecake layer and swirl the two together with a skewer. Bake as indicated, until set and lightly browned. Cool. Refrigerate leftovers.

Serves 24-30

 350° 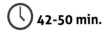 42-50 min.

Banana Cake Bars

Preheat the oven and grease a 10 x 15 x 1" pan. In a large mixing bowl, beat together ½ C. softened butter and 1½ C. sugar on medium speed until creamy. One at a time, add 2 eggs, beating after each addition. Beat in 1 C. sour cream and 1 tsp. vanilla until blended. In a separate bowl, combine 2 C. flour, 1 tsp. baking soda, and ¼ tsp. salt; stir flour mixture into the batter. Mix in 1 C. mashed ripe banana and spread in the prepped pan. Bake as indicated or until cake tests done with a toothpick. Cool completely.

To make the chocolate-peanut butter frosting, stir together 3½ C. powdered sugar and 3 T. unsweetened cocoa powder in a medium bowl. Add ¼ C. creamy peanut butter, ¾ tsp. vanilla, and 6 to 7 T. milk, beating on medium speed until light and smooth. Spread over cooled cake and cut as desired. *Serves 20-24*

 350° 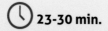 23-30 min.

Cinnamon Crumb Coffee Cake

Cake

1 (15.25 oz.) pkg. yellow
   cake mix
1¼ C. sour cream
⅓ C. vegetable oil
3 eggs
1 tsp. cinnamon
½ tsp. ground nutmeg

Topping

2½ C. flour
½ C. brown sugar
1¼ tsp. cinnamon
¼ tsp. ground nutmeg
1 C. butter, melted

Icing

1 C. sifted powdered sugar
¼ C. sour cream

Preheat the oven and grease and flour a 10 x 15 x 1" pan.

In a large mixing bowl, beat together all the cake ingredients on medium speed until smooth and well combined, about 2 minutes. Pour batter into the prepped pan, spreading evenly, and bake 18 to 20 minutes or until cake tests done with a toothpick.

Meanwhile, combine the topping ingredients in a large bowl until moist and crumbly. Sprinkle over the warm cake and return to the oven for 15 minutes more. Let cool completely.

To make the icing, whisk together powdered sugar and sour cream until smooth. Drizzle over the cooled cake before serving.
Serves 18-24

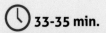 350° 33-35 min.

Banana Cream Slab Pie

Crust

1 (12 oz.) pkg. vanilla wafer cookies, finely crushed (about 3 C.)
½ C. butter, melted

Filling

1 C. sugar
⅓ C. cornstarch
½ tsp. salt
4 C. whole milk

3 eggs
¼ C. butter, sliced
1½ tsp. vanilla
3 or 4 bananas, peeled & sliced

Topping

2 C. heavy cream
⅓ C. sugar
1 tsp. vanilla

 350° 10-12 min.

Preheat the oven. In a medium bowl, stir together the crumbs and melted butter until well mixed. Reserve 3 tablespoons of the crumb mixture for garnishing the finished pie. Firmly press the remaining mixture into the bottom and partway up the sides of a 10 x 15 x 1" pan. Bake the crust as indicated, until lightly browned. Let cool.

For the filling, combine sugar, cornstarch, and salt in a big saucepan. Whisk in the milk and eggs. Place over medium-low heat and slowly bring to a boil, stirring constantly until thickened. Remove from heat and whisk in the sliced butter and vanilla until smooth. Let cool 15 to 20 minutes, then place plastic wrap on the surface of filling and refrigerate to cool completely, about an hour.

When ready to assemble, prepare the topping. In a chilled bowl with chilled beaters, beat the cream on medium-high speed until thickened. Gradually beat in the sugar and vanilla until soft peaks form. Arrange banana slices over the crust. Spread prepared filling over bananas and cover with topping. Refrigerate for 1 hour. Sprinkle with the reserved crumbs before serving. Refrigerate any leftovers. *Serves 15-24*

Quick Tip

*To make a **GRAHAM CRACKER CRUST** for this pie, substitute 3 C. graham cracker crumbs, ¼ C. plus 2 T. sugar, and ⅔ C. melted butter in place of the ingredients listed. Prepare and bake as directed.*

Mississippi Mud Bars

Preheat the oven and grease a 10 x 15 x 1" pan. In a large microwave-safe bowl, combine 1 C. butter and ⅔ C. semi-sweet chocolate chips; microwave for 1 to 2 minutes, stirring every 30 seconds until smooth. Whisk in 2 C. sugar, 1½ C. flour, ½ C. unsweetened cocoa powder, ¾ tsp. salt, 4 eggs, and 1 tsp. vanilla until blended. Spread batter in the prepped pan and bake for 20 minutes. Remove from oven and sprinkle 1 (10.5 oz.) bag mini marshmallows on top. Bake 8 to 12 minutes longer, until golden brown.

To make the frosting, melt ½ C. butter in a saucepan over medium-low heat. Whisk in ⅓ C. unsweetened cocoa powder, ⅓ C. milk, and 1 tsp. vanilla; heat for 1 minute. Whisk in 3¼ C. sifted powdered sugar until smooth. Drizzle frosting over the warm cake and sprinkle with 1 C. toasted pecans. Cool completely and refrigerate before serving. Refrigerate leftovers. *Serves 24-28*

 350°  28-32 min.

Caramel Apple Bars

Preheat the oven and grease a 10 x 15 x 1" pan. Combine 1⅔ C. flour, 1½ C. old-fashioned oats, and ⅔ C. brown sugar in a bowl. Cut in ¾ C. plus 1 T. butter *(sliced)* until crumbly. Set aside ¾ C. of the mixture for the topping and stir in 1 T. sugar; press the remaining mixture into the bottom of the prepped pan. Bake the crust for 10 to 12 minutes, until lightly browned.

For the filling, beat 2 (8 oz.) pkgs. softened cream cheese on medium speed until light and creamy. Mix in 1 C. caramel dip *(we used Marzetti's)*. On low speed, beat in 2 T. brown sugar, 1 T. flour, 1 egg, and 1 tsp. vanilla; pour mixture over warm crust. Peel and chop 2 Granny Smith apples; arrange over cream cheese layer, pressing lightly. Bake 15 to 20 minutes, until set. Sprinkle set-aside topping over apples and broil just until browned. Cool completely, then chill until firm. Drizzle with more caramel dip before serving. Refrigerate leftovers. *Serves 28*

 350°  25-32 min.

Ho-Ho Cake

Cake

¾ C. butter
¼ C. unsweetened
  cocoa powder
¾ C. water
1⅔ C. sugar
1⅔ C. flour
½ tsp. salt
1 tsp. baking soda
6 T. milk
2 eggs
1 tsp. vanilla

Filling

1¼ C. milk
5 T. flour
1 C. sugar
½ C. butter
½ C. shortening
1 tsp. vanilla

Frosting

1 C. sugar
½ C. butter
½ C. milk
1 C. semi-sweet
  chocolate chips

Preheat the oven and grease a 10 x 15 x 1" pan. Combine the first three cake ingredients in a medium saucepan and bring to a boil over medium heat. Remove from heat and whisk in sugar, flour, salt, and baking soda. Add milk, eggs, and vanilla, stirring well. Spread in the prepped pan and bake as indicated. Cool completely.

Meanwhile, make the filling. Combine milk and flour in a small saucepan over low heat and whisk constantly until mixture thickens like pudding, 5 to 10 minutes. Cool to room temperature. In a mixing bowl, beat together sugar, butter, shortening, and vanilla on medium speed for 3 minutes, until light and fluffy. Add the cooled milk mixture and beat on high for 7 minutes. Spread over cake and chill until set.

Combine the first three frosting ingredients in a saucepan over medium heat and boil for 2 minutes. Remove from heat and stir in chocolate chips until melted. Pour over chilled filling layer and refrigerate until set. *Serves 24-32*

 350° 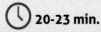 20-23 min.

Cranberry-Orange Cheesecake

Preheat the oven and grease a 10 x 15 x 1" pan. In a bowl, combine 2½ C. graham cracker crumbs, ½ C. finely chopped pecans, 6 T. melted butter, and 3 T. sugar. Press mixture into the bottom of the prepped pan and bake 5 minutes. Let cool.

In a big mixing bowl, beat 3 (8 oz.) pkgs. softened cream cheese until smooth. Beat in 6 T. sugar, 1 T. orange juice, 1 T. orange zest, 2 tsp. vanilla, and optional ¼ tsp. orange extract. One at a time, beat in 4 eggs until blended; fold in 1½ C. sour cream. Spread filling over the crust and bake 20 minutes or until center is firm. Cool completely, then chill at least 2 hours.

For the topping, mix ½ C. sugar, ⅔ C. orange juice, 1 tsp. orange zest, and 3 C. frozen cranberries in a saucepan; simmer over medium-low heat until berries are softened. Mix 2 tsp. cornstarch with 2 T. orange juice and stir into saucepan; boil about 1 minute to thicken. Cool and serve over cheesecake. Refrigerate leftovers. *Serves 18-24*

  350°   25 min.

PB-Carameluscious Bars

Preheat the oven and grease a 10 x 15 x 1" pan. Combine 2¼ C. flour, 1 tsp. baking soda, and 1 tsp. salt in a small bowl. In a large mixing bowl, beat 1 C. softened butter until smooth; beat in ¾ C. sugar, ¾ C. brown sugar, and 1 tsp. vanilla until creamy, then beat in 2 eggs. Gradually beat in the flour mixture until blended and stir in 2 C. semi-sweet chocolate chips. Press ⅔ of the dough into the bottom of the prepped pan and bake 8 to 10 minutes. Remove from oven and set aside.

Combine 60 vanilla caramels and ½ C. evaporated milk in a double boiler; heat until melted, stirring frequently. Remove from heat and stir in ½ C. creamy peanut butter. Pour over warm crust and sprinkle with ½ C. semi-sweet chocolate chips. Drop spoonfuls of remaining dough over the filling in pan. Bake 15 to 20 minutes more, until golden brown and set. Let cool before cutting. *Serves 32-35*

 375°  23-30 min.

Raspberry-Rhubarb Slab Pie

Crust

3¼ C. flour
1 tsp. salt
1 C. butter, sliced
¾ C. plus 1 T. milk
1 egg yolk

Filling

2 C. sugar
⅓ C. cornstarch

6 C. fresh or frozen
unsweetened raspberries
(thawed & drained if frozen)

3 to 4 C. sliced fresh or frozen
rhubarb *(thawed & drained
if frozen)*

Toppings

Egg wash *(see p. 29)*
1¼ C. powdered sugar
½ tsp. vanilla
5 to 6 tsp. milk

For the crust, combine flour and salt in a large bowl; cut in butter until crumbly. Whisk together the milk and egg yolk, then gradually stir into flour mixture until dough comes together. Divide in half, wrap separately in plastic wrap, and refrigerate at least 30 minutes.

When ready to assemble, preheat the oven. Roll out one piece of dough to make a 14 x 19" rectangle. Transfer to a 10 x 15 x 1" pan and press dough into the corners and up the sides, leaving a 1" overhang. To make the filling, mix sugar and cornstarch in a big bowl; add raspberries and rhubarb, tossing well. Spoon filling into the crust.

Roll remaining dough into a rectangle big enough to cover pie; set over filling and trim edges even with the bottom crust. Pinch the layers together and seal with a fork or crimp as desired. Brush top crust with egg wash and cut a few slits in the top. Bake as indicated, until golden brown and bubbly. Cool completely.

Whisk together powdered sugar, vanilla, and milk until smooth. Drizzle over pie before cutting. *Serves 24*

 375° 45-50 min.

Pineapple Dream Dessert

Preheat the oven and grease a 10 x 15 x 1" pan. In a medium bowl, combine 4 C. graham cracker crumbs, ¼ C. sugar, and ⅔ C. melted butter, stirring well. Reserve ⅓ C. crumbs; press the remainder over the bottom and ½" up the sides of the prepped pan. Bake 9 to 12 minutes, until firm; let cool.

Drain 2 (20 oz.) cans crushed pineapple and set fruit aside; discard liquid. In a medium mixing bowl, beat together 1 (8 oz.) pkg. softened cream cheese and 1 C. softened butter on medium speed until smooth and creamy. Gradually beat in 4 C. powdered sugar on low speed until combined; increase speed and beat 1 minute more. Stir in ⅓ C. of the set-aside pineapple; spread over the cooled crust.

Fold remaining pineapple into 1 (12 oz.) container whipped topping *(thawed)*. Spread over cream cheese layer and sprinkle with reserved crumbs. Refrigerate at least 4 hours or overnight. Store any leftovers in the fridge. *Serves 15-24*

 300°   9-12 min.

Cream Puff Caramel Dessert

Preheat the oven and grease a 10 x 15 x 1" pan. In a large saucepan over medium heat, bring 1 C. water and ½ C. butter to a full boil, melting the butter. Stir in 1 C. flour and remove from heat; let cool about 5 minutes. One at a time, add 4 eggs and beat well with a spoon after each addition. Spread dough evenly in the prepped pan and bake as indicated, until puffy and light golden brown. Cool completely, pressing down on the crust if it puffed up during baking.

In a large bowl, combine 3 (3.4 oz.) pkgs. caramel instant pudding mix *(or another flavor)* and whisk together with 4½ C. whole milk until smooth and thick, about 2 minutes. Spread pudding over the cooled crust and then spread 1 (8 or 12 oz.) container whipped topping *(thawed)* over the pudding layer. Chill at least 2 hours. Before serving, drizzle with caramel topping and chocolate syrup.
Serves 20

 375°  25-30 min.

Dutch Apple Slab Pie

Crust

1½ C. flour
1½ T. sugar
¼ tsp. salt
½ tsp. baking powder
½ C. shortening
2 egg yolks, beaten
¼ C. water

Filling

10 C. thinly sliced, peeled
apples (*about 8 large
Granny Smith, Fuji, Golden
Delicious, and/or Honeycrisp
apples*)

1¾ C. sugar
2 T. lemon juice
2 T. flour
1 tsp. cinnamon

Topping

1 C. flour
⅔ C. brown sugar
1 tsp. cinnamon
⅔ C. butter, sliced

To make the crust, mix the flour, sugar, salt, and baking powder in a large bowl. Cut in the shortening until mixture resembles coarse crumbs. Mix egg yolks and water together and stir into the flour mixture until dough forms a ball. Roll out dough on a floured surface to make a 13 x 18" rectangle. Transfer to a 10 x 15 x 1" pan and press dough over the bottom, into the corners, and up the sides; crimp dough around the rim and set aside.

In a large bowl, combine all the filling ingredients. Spread filling in the crust and set aside. Preheat the oven.

To make the topping, combine flour, brown sugar, and cinnamon in a big bowl; cut in the butter until coarse crumbs form. Sprinkle topping over the apples and bake as indicated, until filling is bubbly and crust is golden brown. *Serves 20-24*

350°   55-60 min.

Key Lime-Macadamia Dessert

Preheat the oven and line a 10 x 15 x 1" pan with greased foil. Combine 2¾ C. flour, ⅔ C. brown sugar, ¾ C. chopped macadamia nuts, ½ C. sliced butter, and ½ tsp. salt in a food processor and pulse until finely ground. Press mixture into the prepped pan and bake as indicated or until lightly browned. Cool completely.

In a saucepan over low heat, heat ¾ C. sugar and ½ C. key lime juice until sugar dissolves; remove from heat. Meanwhile, sprinkle 1 (.25 oz.) envelope unflavored gelatin over 2 T. lime juice in a medium bowl; let stand 3 minutes. Add the hot mixture and stir until gelatin dissolves. Whisk in 1 (14 oz.) can sweetened condensed milk and 1 tsp. lime zest. Set the bowl in a bigger bowl filled with ice for 10 minutes, whisking often. Meanwhile, in a chilled bowl with chilled beaters, beat 2½ C. heavy cream until soft peaks form; fold into the gelatin mixture and pour over crust. Chill 8 hours. Garnish with lime zest and more nuts. Refrigerate leftovers. *Serves 20-24*

 350°   20 min.

Chocolate-Mallow Crisp Squares

Preheat the oven and grease a 10 x 15 x 1" pan. In a medium bowl, stir together 1 (16.5 oz.) pkg. chocolate cake mix, ⅓ C. melted butter, and 1 egg until well mixed but crumbly. Press mixture into the prepped pan and bake 12 to 15 minutes, until puffy and set. Remove from oven and sprinkle with 3 C. mini marshmallows. Return to oven for 2 minutes more.

Meanwhile, in a large saucepan over low heat, combine 1 (10 oz.) pkg. peanut butter chips, ⅔ C. light corn syrup, ¼ C. creamy peanut butter, and 1 tsp. vanilla, stirring until melted and smooth. Remove from heat and stir in 1½ to 2 C. crisp rice cereal and 2 C. chopped salted peanuts. Immediately spoon the mixture over the marshmallow layer. Let cool before cutting.

Serves 28-36

 350°  14-17 min.

Caramel Praline Sheet Cake

Pralines

1½ C. chopped pecans
¾ C. brown sugar

Cake

½ C. butter
½ C. shortening
1 C. water
2 C. brown sugar
½ C. buttermilk
½ tsp. baking soda

2 eggs
1 tsp. vanilla
2 C. flour

Frosting

6 T. butter
½ C. heavy cream
1 C. brown sugar
2 C. powdered sugar, sifted
2 tsp. vanilla

 400°  18-20 min.

To make pralines, place pecans in a skillet over medium-high heat and cook 1 to 2 minutes, stirring constantly. Add brown sugar and stir constantly until sugar melts and coats the pecans. Dump onto parchment paper and separate the nuts while they cool.

Preheat the oven and grease a 10 x 15 x 1" pan. For the cake, combine butter, shortening, and water in a medium saucepan and bring to a boil over medium heat. Remove from heat and pour into a large mixing bowl. Stir in the brown sugar until dissolved. Stir in the buttermilk, then add the baking soda, eggs, and vanilla and whisk until well blended. Mix in the flour until smooth. Pour batter into the prepped pan and bake as indicated or until cake tests done with a toothpick. Let cool.

Make the frosting by heating the butter, cream, and brown sugar in a medium saucepan over medium heat until mixture comes to a boil, stirring often. Remove from heat and whisk in the powdered sugar and vanilla. Pour frosting evenly over the cake and sprinkle with the prepped pralines. *Serves 20*

Quick Tip

*To **TEST CAKES** for doneness, poke a toothpick or wooden skewer into the center and if it comes out clean (or with just a few small crumbs), set it on a cooling rack. If batter sticks to it, bake it a few more minutes and retest until done. Another sign to look for: the cake's edges will start to pull away from the pan.*

Oreo Refrigerator Slab Pie

Crust

1½ (14.3 oz.) pkgs. chocolate
 Oreos *(about 45 cookies)*
½ C. butter, melted

Filling

2 (8 oz.) pkgs. cream
 cheese, softened
½ C. sugar
2 (3.4 oz.) pkgs. chocolate
 instant pudding mix

2 C. milk
1 (8 oz.) container whipped
 topping, thawed

Toppings

½ (14.3 oz.) pkg. chocolate
 Oreos *(18-20 cookies)*
1 (8 oz.) container whipped
 topping, thawed
Fudge sauce, optional

Preheat the oven. For the crust, place cookies in a food processor and process until fine crumbs form. Transfer to a large bowl and stir in the butter. Press the crumb mixture into the bottom and partway up the sides of a 10 x 15 x 1" pan. Bake as indicated, until set. Let cool completely.

To make the filling, beat together the cream cheese and sugar on medium speed until smooth. Add pudding mixes and gradually beat in the milk until creamy and smooth. Fold in the whipped topping until well blended. Spread filling over the cooled crust and refrigerate 2 to 3 hours, until set.

For the toppings, cut 10 cookies in half and crush the remaining cookies. Stir the crushed cookies into the whipped topping and spread over the dessert. Garnish the top with the halved cookies, and if you'd like, drizzle with a little fudge sauce. Serve cold and store leftovers in the fridge. *Serves 20*

Index

Quick Tips